£2.75

Focus On
South African
STEAM

Roger Siviter

DAVID & CHARLES
NEWTON ABBOT   LONDON   NORTH POMFRET (VT)

CONTENTS

British Library Cataloguing in Publication Data

Siviter, Roger
    Focus on South African steam.
    1. Locomotives – South Africa
    I. Title
    625.2'61'0968   TJ603.4.A435

    ISBN 0–7153–8087–7

Library of Congress Catalog Card Number 80–85495

© Roger Siviter 1981

Photoset by Northern Phototypesetting Co, Bolton
and printed in Great Britain
by Biddles Ltd, Guildford
for David & Charles (Publishers) Limited
Brunel House Newton Abbot Devon

Published in the United States of America
by David & Charles Inc
North Pomfret Vermont 05053 USA

Published in Canada
by Douglas David & Charles Limited
1875 Welch Street North Vancouver BC

INTRODUCTION

With working steam having finished in many parts of the world by the late 1960s and early 1970s, many enthusiasts who normally would not have travelled abroad to see and photograph steam suddenly became aware that the sight, sound and fury of working steam was still in abundance in countries like South Africa. Much credit for this must go to people like David Thornhill of *World Steam* for the very informative booklet *Steam in South Africa and Rhodesia*, and the many others who regularly contribute to *World Steam* bulletins, and also to the *Continental Railway Journal*.

There are, moreover, a large number of enthusiasts in South Africa itself which means that many engines are being preserved. Each year special trains, like the Sunset Limited, are organised which run for up to ten days, using a wide variety of engines, and are usually very successful. There is also talk of such lines as George to Knysna being preserved. Thus the steam scene in South Africa offers much to the enthusiast and this book, apart from portraying steam in action in the album sections, also serves as a guide to the railway enthusiast visiting South Africa in search of working steam.

There are still many areas left where a fair quantity of steam can be found and in the following pages I have set out what are considered to be the remaining principal centres as at the beginning of the 1980s where steam locomotives are still in operation and also the photographic possibilities of each area.

In the illustrated section of the book, I have tried to show a balanced selection of photographs covering the present areas of steam working. I hope the reader will forgive me for including a few retrospective pictures of locomotives and lines which are now almost completely dieselised. All the photographs were taken with Nikon cameras and lenses, using Ilford film developed in Aculux and printed on Kentmere paper.

I should like to thank my wife Christina for all the hours of work she has given me in the preparation of this book, and Joan Wappett for the typing. Also, I must thank all the people of South African Railways for all the help and assistance given to me on my visits.

November 1980   Roger Siviter

1. *Frontispiece:* A pair of Class 25NC 4–8–4s, led by 3433 *Heather*, storm out of Poupan with a Kimberley–De Aar goods on 28 July 1980.

2. *Left:* Grahamstown shed on 28 July 1979 with Class 19D No 2750.

3. *Left:* Pulling out of Sekonyela on 30 July 1980 is a Bloemfontein/Bethlehem passenger train headed by Class 25NC No 3403, built by North British in 1954. This location is about eight miles north of Ficksburg.

4. *Bottom left:* A pair of Class 15AR 4–8–2s, Nos 2022 and 1849, near Kortaf with a Burgersdorp–Aliwal North goods on 5 August 1976. This line together with the famous Aliwal North to Barkly East line has now been dieselised.

5. *Below:* Contrast between locomotive and striking rock formation behind as Class 25NC 4–8–4 No 3410 *Bethlehem* drifts slowly towards the passing loop at Sekonyela, north of Ficksburg with a Bethlehem to Bloemfontein goods on 30 July 1980.

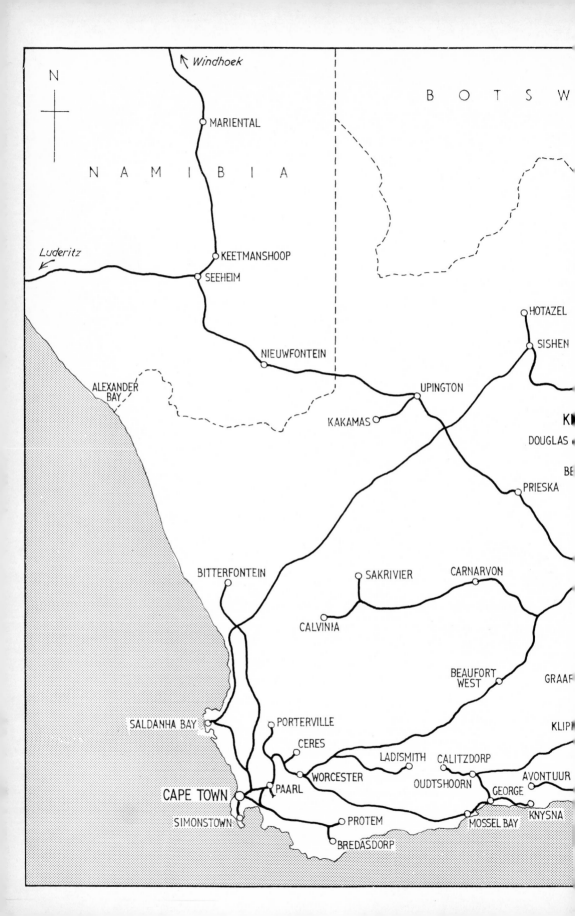

PLANNING AN ITINERARY

Many airlines, including British Airways, Lufthansa, KLM, and of course South African Airways have regular flights to and from South Africa. Nearly all flights terminate at Johannesburg, where the visitor can connect with a large number of internal flights to all the main cities and towns.

As South Africa is a large country and steam workings at the moment are spread fairly evenly over a wide area, the enthusiast could easily waste time and petrol on unnecessary travel. To help him make the best use of his time, I have worked out some itineraries which take in the main steam lines, starting at convenient air terminals. For example, one could take an internal flight from Johannesburg to Kimberley, a saving of something approaching 300 miles and then work on this route:

Itinerary One

1 Kimberley to De Aar (to include the Springfontein-Koffiefontein branch).
2 George-Knysna branch.
3 Avontuur-Assegaaibos (2ft gauge).
4 Port Elizabeth for Suburban and Apple Express.
5 Grahamstown area.
6 Sterkstroom-Maclear branch.
7 Bloemfontein-Bethlehem.
8 Into Natal for 2ft gauge and industrial in northern Natal.
9 Transvaal area.

Another way which is very popular is to fly from Johannesburg to Port Elizabeth, a distance of 650 miles and then follow this route:

Itinerary Two

1 Port Elizabeth to Assegaaibos for 2ft gauge line to Avontuur.
2 George-Knysna Branch.
3 Back to Port Elizabeth for Suburban and Apple Express.
4 Grahamstown area.
5 Sterkstroom-Maclear branch.
6 De Aar-Kimberley (including Springfontein-Koffiefontein branch).

From then on as Itinerary One starting at 7 Bloemfontein-Bethlehem.

I estimate that between 21 and 24 clear days should cover either of these two itineraries. Visitors with one or two days less could miss out, for example, part of the Natal 2ft gauge and some industrial lines, but obviously this would be up to enthusiasts' own preferences.

One very important point to bear in mind is that the Apple Express only runs during a certain time of the year and only on Saturdays. Therefore, the enthusiast who wants either to travel on or photograph this train must make sure that his itinerary enables him to be in Port Elizabeth by Friday evening for the train on Saturday morning.

For people with much less time, perhaps a period of around 14 days, I suggest flying to Kimberley as for the first itinerary then use the following route:

Itinerary Three

1 Kimberley-De Aar.
2 Springfontein-Koffiefontein.
3 Bloemfontein-Bethlehem.
4 Umzinto-Donnybrook and Estcourt-Weenan (2ft gauge).
5 Northern Natal industrial.
6 Transvaal area.

On all of these itineraries there are a few days when longer distances will have to be covered but in general the journeys are quite comfortable, allowing plenty of time to see steam.

I have not recommended any length of time that the enthusiast should spend on a certain line, because I feel that personal preference is important. Indeed many will want to travel behind steam. Some lines are busier than others, some are more scenic and on other lines, by using a car, it is possible to follow a train for most of its journey. The reader will find information regarding these aspects in the details of principal steam lines on pages 18 to 29.

These itineraries are meant only as suggestions, but I would advise any enthusiast to have some sort of plan before setting out. Please also remember that with the gradual demise of steam in

South Africa, it would be as well to check on the steam workings of an area before starting a journey to that particular region. This sort of information can usually be obtained at the main locomotive depots along the route.

Internal Travel and Car Hire

Having once arrived at his starting point in South Africa and bearing in mind that most trains are slow and infrequent, the visitor will find that the hired car is the most convenient method of transport to get to the most scenic locations. After all whatever the attractions of travelling by train it is often not possible to get far away from stations other than by walking even if the service is sufficiently frequent to make a location worthwhile. Most of the big car hire firms have offices in the major cities and airports.

A further point is that a visitor needs an international driving licence to drive in South Africa.

Permits

Before visiting South Africa, it is important to obtain permission for photography and visits to sheds etc; this is done by writing to:

The General Manager's Office,
South African Railways,
Johannesburg Station,
Johannesburg.

The usual indemnity forms are required to be signed and sent back, so it is important to allow plenty of time.

Time of the Year to go

Remember that the seasons in South Africa are the opposite to the northern hemisphere; summer in Europe or North America is winter in South Africa. Also, remember that the sun, after rising in the east, circles to the north.

The two most popular periods in which enthusiasts visit South Africa are March and April (Autumn) and May through to September (Winter). I personally think that the latter period is the best time of year for photography, the days usually being very bright and cloudless, and the sun is not too high at midday. There is a bonus in the cold early mornings which means good steam and smoke effects.

Hotels

There are many hotels in all the areas covered by this book but my advice is that in some of the smaller towns, for example, Sterkstroom, it is as well to book accommodation beforehand (say 24 hours), not only to secure a room but to give the hotel time to prepare meals etc. In some places like Kraankuil on the De Aar to Kimberley line, the town more or less consists of the hotel, shop and the station!

Railway Timetables

Timetables can be bought at most large stations in South Africa.

Maps

The South African Tourist Board publishes two maps: one is a fold-up sheet which shows all the main roads, railways, etc; the second is in the form of a booklet and divides the country into eight sections showing much more detail than the first map as well as street plans of the major cities. Also included is a very useful index of towns, villages, etc. Both maps are available at South African Tourist Offices.

Late Changes

In a book recording events at a specific time it is inevitable that changes will occur, usually with the introduction of modern traction on certain services or lines, but even while this book was in preparation it appears that the Burgersdorp-Rosmead line in the Northern Cape, after being almost completely dieselised, has partially reverted to steam traction and now sees several trains a day usually hauled by 15ARs. This also means that engines from Burgersdorp still need to go to Queenstown for washout, necessitating, on the return journey, the long climb over Boesmanshoek Pass. This very photogenic spot is situated on the main line from East London, a few miles north of Sterkstroom from which place a road follows the line almost to the top of the pass.

GUIDE TO PRINCIPAL
STEAM LOCOMOTIVE DEPOTS

Port Elizabeth, Sydenham
This shed is situated adjacent to Sydenham station which is about two miles out of Port Elizabeth on the main suburban line to Swartkops.

Port Elizabeth, Humewood Road (2ft gauge)
The shed is adjacent to the 2ft gauge station, terminus of Apple Express.

Johannesburg, Germiston
To get to the shed turn left outside Germiston station, walk along Station Street and continue into Railway Street. The shed entrance is a subway at the end of a short cul-de-sac on the left.

Grahamstown
This shed is approximately 200yd from the station platforms on the line to Port Alfred.

De Aar
The shed is situated to the east of the main line to Beaufort West at the southern end of the station about a quarter of a mile from the platforms.

George
This small sub shed of Voorbaai is located a few yards from the western end of the station.

Kimberley, Beaconsfield
The shed is situated by Beaconsfield station which is off Free State Road, approximately two miles from the centre of the city.

Pretoria, Capitol Park
This shed is about 2½ miles north of Pretoria station. Follow Paul Kruger Street towards Pretoria North and the shed entrance is on the right between two rail over-bridges.

Port Shepstone (mixed gauge)
Depot is adjacent to the station.

Umzinto (2ft gauge)
This shed is adjacent to the station.

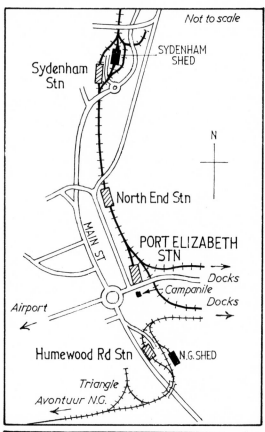

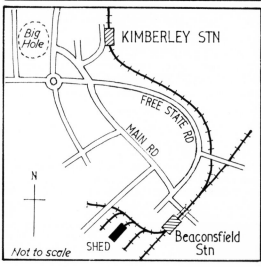

Assegaaibos (2ft gauge)
The shed is situated by the line to Avontuur about a quarter of a mile from the station. An interesting feature of this shed is the turntable, unusual for South African depots.

Avontuur (2ft gauge)
This shed lies behind the station.

Estcourt (2ft gauge)
The shed is situated in the junction of the line to Weenan (2ft gauge) and the main line to Ladysmith.

Waterval Boven
This shed is situated to the east of the station about a quarter of a mile from the end of the platform.

Breyton
Shed is near to station just off the line to Waterval Boven.

Bloemfontein
The shed is away from the main station and the accompanying map shows the route from the station.

Bethlehem
Turn left out of the station along Cambridge Street then turn left into McNicol Street, cross over the line and turn right into Joubert Street. The shed entrance is on the right-hand side. It is approximately 15 minutes walk from the station to the depot.

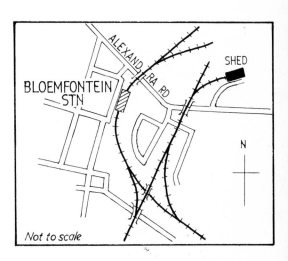

STEAM LOCOMOTIVE CLASSES TODAY

South African steam motive power has always offered a variety of types from many builders and many countries. Indeed, locomotive designs were remarkably cosmopolitan, showing affinities not only with Britain but also the engineering schools of several European countries, Canada and the USA, blending well to form the domestic South African types. South Africa did not have a major locomotive building industry of its own either privately or on SAR, and designs originating from SAR chief mechanical engineers were usually constructed by private industry in other countries although in some cases engines were built abroad and erected in South Africa. Sometimes major components for one type came from several countries. Despite the adoption of 3ft 6in gauge (Cape gauge) for most lines, size and power have been anything but small. A few SAR classes are larger and more powerful than comparable types on 4ft $8\frac{1}{2}$in gauge in Britain and Europe. Yet despite having a narrow 'standard' gauge, even narrower 2ft gauge tracks run long distances in the Cape and Natal, some of which retain steam haulage at present. Here again the small gauge does not mean small engines and some of SAR's 2ft gauge Garratts are the most powerful engines of the gauge in the world, and are much larger than British 2ft gauge types, being higher, longer, and, in a few cases, almost four times the gauge width instead of the more usual three times.

Once a large user of Beyer-Garratt articulated locomotives and their derivatives, SAR has concentrated on maintaining rigid-frame types for the last years of steam, largely because the more difficult lines for which the Garratts were built have been dieselised or electrified. Now, the once mighty Garratts on the 3ft 6in gauge are a declining breed although some former SAR Garratts have recently been transferred to Zimbabwe.

Although a few older types can still be found on isolated duties the following are the principal classes which are still at work in any quantity.

Class 12A and 12AR 4–8–2

The Class 12A 4–8–2s were designed by D. A. Hendrie, SAR's chief mechanical engineer from 1910 to 1922, and introduced in 1919. They were a development of the Class 12 of 1912, at the time of its introduction the largest rigid-frame type in South Africa, but had a combustion chamber addition to the firebox which effectively reduced the length of the Class 12 long firetubes. The 12As had larger cylinders at 24in diameter by 26in stroke instead of the $22\frac{1}{2}$in stroke of the Class 12s. With boiler pressure of 190lb and coupled wheel diameter of 4ft 3in, tractive effort was over 41,800lb, ideal for the Witbank-Germiston coal workings for which both types were designed. A total of 67 Class 12A locomotives were built between 1919 and 1929, divided between North British Locomotive Co in Scotland and Henschel & Sohn in Germany. From 1943 Class 12As were gradually rebuilt with large diameter standard boilers having a round-top firebox, becoming Class 12AR; not all engines were dealt with and examples of both types survive, the unrebuilt engines being almost the last SAR type to retain Belpaire fireboxes. Most of the 12ARs are now based in the Transvaal and locomotives of both classes are today confined mainly to heavy shunting.

Class 15A and 15AR 4–8–2

The Class 15 locomotives were originally introduced in 1913 for mixed-traffic duties in the Orange Free State but like the Class 12 the length of their boilers led to problems with long firetubes; the type was soon redesigned with a combustion chamber to reduce tube length and classed as 15A. It became one of the best main line mixed-traffic classes in South Africa. Class 15A locomotives were built over a period of 11 years from 1914 to 1925 by three manufacturers, North British and Beyer, Peacock in Britain, and Maffei in Germany. During the 1930s, in common with railways in many parts of the world, and which Churchward of the British GWR had realised 30 years before, SAR found the multiplicity of locomotive types

and boiler variations were resulting in high maintenance costs. As a result a range of standard boilers was devised, including the No 2A, which was fitted to both Classes 15 and 15A which became an identical Class 15AR. At 5ft $7\frac{1}{2}$in inside diameter, the new boilers were nearly 3in larger than the originals, and the slightly increased 190lb/sq in pressure raised the tractive effort to 33,880lb. The 15ARs, some of which are more than 55 years old can still be found at Port Elizabeth and a few other places.

Class 15CA 4–8–2

In the mid 1920s SAR looked across the Atlantic to North America for its next locomotives with two designs, a mixed traffic 4–8–2 the 15C and an express passenger 4–6–2 the 16D. The 15Cs were supplied by Baldwin and erected at Salt River workshops at Cape Town. These engines brought many American features to SAR including bar frames instead of traditional British plate frames, such improved boiler fittings as top-feed, self cleaning smokeboxes, and grease lubrication. It was soon found, though, that the frames were cracking near the front of the firebox and a new design was prepared in which the frames were widened under the firebox. The revised design was introduced in 1926 being designated 15CA while the original Baldwin engines became 15CB. The first batch of 15CAs was built by the American Locomotive Co (Alco) and the second lot by Baldwin, but the total order was shared around several countries and further batches to the same American design were built by North British Locomotive Co and Breda. Visually the 15CAs were totally different from the traditionally British style 15s and 15As with high, slightly tapering boilers having a backward slope on the top of the firebox, the squat boiler mountings, the high running plate well above the wheels and motion, much of the plumbing exposed on the outside of the boiler, and the high-sided tenders carrying 14 tons of coal and 6000 gallons of water compared with the 10 tons and 4250 gallons of the original Class 15 tenders. In recent years since electrification of the Pretoria-Witbank line the 80 engines of the class have been in Eastern Transvaal but the survivors are now virtually confined to shunting and local trip working.

Class 15E and 15F 4–8–2

In 1935 A. G. Watson, who was chief mechanical

engineer in the first half of the 1930s, developed a new design of 4–8–2 based on the 15CA type and classified as 15E, though with a higher pitched boiler to within a few inches of the maximum 13ft height permitted by the loading gauge, meaning just the bare minimum of dome appearing above the boiler and a very squat chimney, the appearance was much more massive. An essential difference was the use of rotary cam valve gear. The addition of large smoke deflectors offset any likeness to the designs of North America even though many American features were retained. They were built by Robert Stephenson & Co in Britain and by Henschel and Berliner Maschinenbau in Germany. Three years after their introduction further locomotives of this type were ordered but with Walschaerts valve gear and classified 15F. The 15Fs became numerically the largest SAR class with 255 locomotives, built over a 10 year period in 1938/9 and 1944/8 by Berliner Maschinenbau and Henschel in 1938 with the rest by North British and Beyer Peacock. The 15Fs are still well in evidence on surviving steam services between Kimberley, Bloemfontein and Bethlehem.

Class 19D 4–8–2
In 1928 came the first of the Class 19 engines, a lightweight 4–8–2 for branch line duties on light track with a maximum axle load of less than 14 tons compared with the roundly 17–18 tons of SAR's main line engines. The long low boilers were

reminiscent of the British products of pre first world war days, but there the resemblance ended for they had high running plates and bar frames from US practice. The initial engines were built by Berliner Maschinenbau. A year later the design was developed into an even lighter type, Class 19A, with axle loadings mainly below 13 tons, brought about by a smaller diameter boiler, reduced cylinder diameter and smaller driving wheels of 4ft 3in instead of 4ft 6in. This time the Swiss Locomotive Works at Winterthur were the builders. In 1930 more branch line 4–8–2s were ordered from Berliner Maschinenbau, with improvements and detail modifications from the original Class 19, known as the 19B. Four years later another batch was ordered from North British but were equipped with rotary cam poppet valve gear and were designated Class 19C. During the tenure of W. A. J. Day as CME in the second half of the 1930s more batches were ordered with detailed variations but with a reversion to Walschaerts valve gear and these were known as Class 19D. Orders were placed with several German builders before the second world war and British firms afterwards, the last batch of 50 from North British Locomotive Co in 1948 having long tenders known as the Vanderbilt type based on USA types with circular water tanks, carrying 6500 gallons and a 12-ton coal bunker on top at the front. Indeed the tenders were longer than the locomotives and were carried on two six-wheeled bogies. It is the 19D with tender variations, that

6. Class 19D 4–8–2 No 2750, a lightweight type with an axleload of less than 14 tons for branch work.

survives in SAR today on a number of branch services.

Class 24 2–8–4

In 1948 came a new type of lightweight branch line locomotive with a 2–8–4 wheel arrangement, new to South Africa. Known as Class 24 they were intended to replace older turn of the century types on specific branches in many parts of South Africa and, in particular, South West Africa, and with a maximum axle load of $11\frac{1}{2}$ tons were designed to run on 45lb/yd rail. In all, 100 were built by North British. Principal advance was in the use of one-piece cast steel frames and cylinders which reduced maintenance costs. They were paired with Vanderbuilt type tenders similar in style but shorter and of lower capacity than those supplied at the same period with the North British built Class 19Ds. The Class 24s also survive for use on specific branches.

Class 25 4–8–4

Steam locomotives in several parts of South Africa have always been at a disadvantage because of the shortage or unsuitability of the water. On the Cape Town-Johannesburg main line it was a particular problem across the Karoo where transportable water tanks had to be taken to watering points in the dry season. In 1950 SAR experimented with condensing equipment on a Class 20 2–10–2 which showed such tremendous water savings that a new type of locomotive with condensing apparatus was evolved for heavy main line duties. This was the Class 25 which turned out to be the last rigid frame 3ft 6in gauge steam locomotives to be built for SAR. Yet they also incorporated many modern design features not seen before in South Africa including roller bearing axleboxes and welded fireboxes. They were also fitted with mechanical stokers. The condensing equipment was in the massive tender which was about 8ft longer than the locomotive and weighed nearly 114 tons against the 120 tons of the locomotive alone. They were truly massive machines, right up to the 13ft height and 10ft width limit of the loading gauge. Visually they were distinguished by a pearshaped smokebox front from which the exhaust steam was taken by a duct to the tender to condense back to water and joined on the way by pipes carrying steam blown off from the safety valves and brake systems. A blower fan driven by an exhaust steam turbine was fitted in the smokebox to create the draught necessary to draw the fire and thus there were no puffs of exhaust steam when the locomotives were on the move. Of the total of 90 25C (condensing) locomotives one was built by Henschel and the rest by North British. Another 50 locomotives, known as 25NC, were built without condensing equipment and with large conventional-style tenders carrying 18 tons of coal and over 10,000 gallons of water.

Following electrification of the main line across the Karoo from the south to De Aar in the early 1970s there has been no need to maintain the condensing apparatus and the 25Cs have gradually been rebuilt without the equipment. Both rebuilt 25Cs and 25NCs survive and are used on both fast passenger and heavy freight services; today they must rank as one of the most powerful surviving rigid frame types in the world. Rebuilt condensing Class 25s work most of the traffic between De Aar and Kimberley and 25NCs from Kimberley to Bloemfontein and Bethlehem.

Class GMA 4–8–2+2–8–4T

South African Railways has always been an extensive user of articulated locomotives, at first of the Mallet type and from the first world war the Beyer-Garratt type, since when numerous Garratt types, not always built by Beyer, Peacock in Britain, and several Garratt variations have been introduced. The main advantages of the Garratt are its ability to provide a powerful locomotive able to run round sharp curves on light track, and ideal on many SAR lines. Sadly today the Garratt is fast becoming a thing of the past in South Africa. The last Garratts to be built for SAR were the GMA, GMAM and GO 4–8–2+2–8–4Ts, all inter-related and based on the 1930s GM type for branch service. The GMA and GMAM types were similar except for differences in coal and water capacities. Indeed some GMAs were converted to GMAM and vice versa. With a maximum axle load of $15\frac{3}{4}$ tons they could work on 60lb/yd rail. The GO used many interchangeable components as, for example, main frames, but had smaller diameter boilers and smaller cylinders to keep the axle load to under $13\frac{1}{2}$ tons for use on 45lb rail. All ran permanently coupled to a supplementary water tank and all had mechanical stokers. Now only a few GMAs remain as the last 3ft 6in gauge Garratts on SAR. From 1975 the class worked almost all trains from Riversdale through George and over the Montagu pass to Oudtshoorn, on the route from Cape Town to Port Elizabeth, but diesels took over in 1980. Some of the GMAs have gone to Zimbabwe although a few survive at Waterval Boven in the Transvaal.

Class NG15 2–8–2s (2ft gauge)
Although SAR 3ft 6in gauge lines are narrow compared with standard or wider gauges in other parts of the world SAR also operates some 2ft gauge lines which in the past have seen a variety of locomotive types. Now there are effectively only two 2ft gauge steam classes left, one of which is the NG15 2–8–2. This class can trace its origin to a German design used by the Otavi Mining Co in what had been German South West Africa from 1922 later transferred to the SAR as Class NG5 and used on the Avontuur line. The NG15s were built over a period of 24 years in four batches from 1931 to 1953, the first by Henschel and the others by Franco-Belge, totalling 16 engines. A further five locomotives of the same type were bought by SAR from the Tsumeb Corporation in 1959. Although built for service in South West Africa, with the conversion of the Otavi line to 3ft 6in gauge by 1960 the NG15s were transferred to the Avontuur line and its two branches where they are in sole command.

Class NGG13 and NGG16 2–6–2+2–6–2T
These two classes, which initially were identical except that the NGG13s had plain bearings and the 16s roller bearings on the carrying axles, became the main type of Garratt locomotive for SAR narrow gauge lines. They had a maximum axle loading of just under 7 tons and could run on 35lb/yd rail. They were built over a period of 40 years and the last were the final Garratts to be built anywhere in the world. International suppliers had a hand in the orders, ranging from Hanomag in 1927, Cockerill (Belgium) in 1937, Beyer, Peacock before and after the second world war and finally Hunslet through their associates in South Africa, Hunslet Taylor, for the last batch in 1967/8. Also included in Class NGG16 are some basically similar engines, differing in many details, built by Beyer, Peacock for the Tsumeb Corporation but delivered new to SAR. This batch had the rear tender unit arranged for coal only and ran permanently coupled to a separate water tank like the GMA Garratts. Now the NGG16s and the few NGG13s are confined to the five narrow gauge lines in Natal, having been displaced from the Avontuur line by the introduction of diesels at the Port Elizabeth end of the line in 1973.

Dimensions of principal SAR steam classes in service 1980

Class	Introduced	Length over couplers	Height	Weight w.o. Engine	Weight w.o. Tender	TE 75%	Boiler Pressure	Driving Wheel Diameter	Cyl. dia. x str.
12A 4–8–2	1919	66′ 11$\frac{5}{8}$″	12′ 10″	99t 1c	51t 1c	41,840lb	190lb/sq in	4′ 3″	24″ x 26″
12AR 4–8–2	1943†	69′ 7″	13′ 0″	99t 5c	66t 0c	41,840lb	190lb/sq in	4′ 3″	24″ x 26″
15AR 4–8–2	1935†	68′ 9$\frac{3}{8}$″	12′ 11$\frac{3}{4}$″	94t 6c	50t 18c	33,880lb	190lb/sq in	4′ 9″	22″ x 28″
15CA 4–8–2	1926	73′ 3$\frac{1}{4}$″	12′ 10″	103t 7c	69t 8c	42,440lb	200lb/sq in	4′ 9″	24″ x 28″
15F 4–8–2	1938	73′ 6″	12′ 11$\frac{1}{2}$″	113t 6c	69t 8c	42,340lb	210lb/sq in	5′ 0″	24″ x 28″
19D 4–8–2	1937	86′ 2$\frac{3}{8}$″*	12′ 10$\frac{3}{8}$″	79t 12c	73t 7c	31,850lb	200lb/sq in	4′ 6″	21″ x 26″
24 2–8–4	1948	74′ 9$\frac{1}{4}$″	12′ 10$\frac{7}{8}$″	72t 18c	56t 11c	27,600lb	200lb/sq in	4′ 3″	19″ x 26″
25NC 4–8–4	1953	91′ 6$\frac{1}{2}$″	13′ 0″	117t 9c	105t 11c	45,360lb	225lb/sq in	5′ 0″	24″ x 28″
GMA 4–8–2+2–8–4T	1954	93′ 10″	13′ 0″	187t 1c		60,700lb	200lb/sq in	4′ 6″	(4) 20$\frac{1}{2}$″ x 26″
NG15 2–8–2	1931	54′ 3$\frac{1}{8}$″	10′ 5″	67t 16c		16,610lb	171lb/sq in	2′ 9$\frac{7}{8}$″	15$\frac{3}{4}$″ x 17$\frac{3}{4}$″
NGG 13 & 16 2–6–2+2–6–2T	1927	48′ 5$\frac{1}{4}$″	10′ 4″	59t 2c		18,850lb	180lb/sq in	2′ 9″	(4) 12″ x 16″

* With Vanderbilt tender.
† Date reboilered.

PRINCIPAL STEAM LINES

General Note

This section covers the principal areas of steam operation left in South Africa, but there are a few other areas where a small number of steam locomotives are still used for shunting and occasional trip working. One such area is Cape Town, but it is not sufficiently important to warrant inclusion, because it is now too sparse and isolated from the main steam areas. A number of branches have not been included for the same reason and for the fact that there is perhaps only one return working a day.

Section 1 — Kimberley-De Aar

This line is part of the Johannesburg-Cape Town trunk route and is the only section on which steam workings remain. The line, 147 miles in length, is double track throughout and is worked by Class 25NCs, mainly rebuilt former condensing locomotives from both Beaconsfield (Kimberley) and De Aar sheds. Many trains are double-headed. De Aar staff have embellished many of their locomotives with girls' names displayed on the smokebox doors.

On leaving Kimberley, the first important place we come to is Modder River. Here is an excellent place for photographing northbound and southbound trains. Northbound trains face a steep climb out of the station and early morning usually sees a fine display of smoke and steam effects. There is a road bridge just south of the station which is a good place to photograph southbound trains, freight trains often being held in the station loop to allow passenger trains through.

A few miles south of Modder River, the main road runs by the line and it is possible in the afternoon, with the sun in the north-west, to obtain panned shots of northbound trains against a background of high trees, the line here descending to Modder River, which means northbound trains are usually running at a fairly brisk pace.

Next we move on to Belmont, where there is a well-kept station on a steep rising grade in the northbound direction. A good position for both morning and evening shots is a crossing about a quarter of a mile north of the station. Other good shots are of trains in both directions coming through the station. From Belmont in a north-

westerly direction is a branch to Douglas on which there is a daily steam working.

Roughly midway on the line is Orange River where all steam trains stop to clean fires and take water. Some of them occasionally shunt in the station and yard. Trains in both directions face steep gradients on leaving the station so there are several good photographic locations in and around this area.

Next we move to Kraankuil, a convenient place to stop and perhaps use as a base for a couple of days, the hotel here being almost on the lineside. Trains tend to move at a brisk rate through the station, but they can be seen for quite a long way in both directions. There are also some fine semaphore signals in and around the station area. These SAR semaphores look rather like British lower quadrant types with spectacles reminiscent of the CLC having top and bottom glasses evenly arranged above and below the arm. Nevertheless the arms work in the upper quadrant so that the red glass is at the bottom of the spectacle casting.

Moving on, we come to Poupan where, from the adjacent main road, very pleasant evening shots are possible of northbound trains leaving the station.

The next important place is Potfontein, where about half a mile north of the station the line runs through a rock cutting and good shots of trains in both directions are possible. There are also some fine signals south of the station which make for further good photographs.

Between Kraankuil and Houtkraal, the next station southbound, a dirt road runs alongside the track for a good distance, making it possible for cine photographers to pace a train, assuming there is a second person to drive the car.

After leaving Houtkraal, there is little of note until reaching the busy railway town of De Aar, where a visit to the locomotive shed is very worthwhile. Apart from the engines in normal service many preserved types are stored here.

Section 1a — Koffiefontein-Springfontein Branch

There are two or three branch lines in the Orange Free State still worked by steam but probably the most interesting is this line of approximately 90

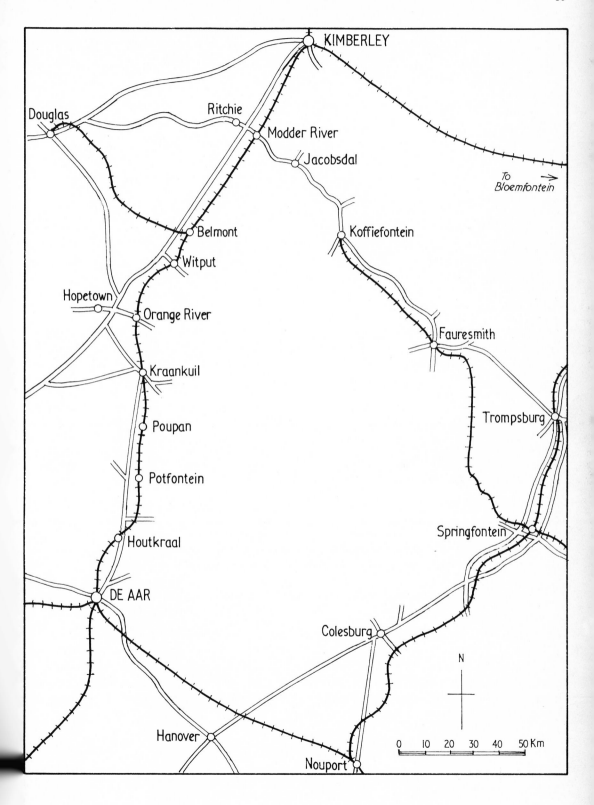

7. Class 24 No 3622 emerges from the shadows into the sunlight as it is about to cross the Kaaimans River bridge with the midday George to Knysna train on 25 July 1979.

miles, worked by Class 19D locomotives. There is a mixed train at 09.40 (not Suns.) and a goods on weekdays only between Fauresmith and Springfontein. One of the attractions of this line is the town of Fauresmith, where on leaving for Springfontein, the train faces a steep climb through the main street, moving so slowly that you could almost follow it on foot. At the top of the main street, is a preserved Class 8B 4–8–0 on a traffic island.

(See photographs Nos. 1, 11, 23, 25, 34, 41, 42, 43, 55, 56, 58, 60, 66, 68, 88, 93, 94, 95.)

Section 2 – George-Knysna Branch

Running from the junction of George on the Cape Town-Port Elizabeth line, this 42 mile long branch line is famous among enthusiasts both for its scenery and the immaculately-kept engines, all of which are Class 24s of Voorbaai, sub-shedded at George. In places the line skirts the Indian Ocean as well as crossing many rivers and tributaries, and also runs through valleys and woods.

The present advertised times of the service are 06.50 and 11.45 from George and 05.40 and 11.30 from Knysna (Sundays excepted), but in practice the 11.45 and 05.40 tend to run later than advertised. It is not too difficult to follow a train by car, one idea being to follow a train from George to roughly halfway, then pick up the return working from Knysna.

The main road from George to Knysna crosses or runs near to the line in many places and, as it is a reasonably short branch, it is worth looking out for possible locations along the line by car beforehand. A word of warning however for if you follow the line after Wilderness, you need to take a dirt road for the first two miles or so to a point where road and rail are combined on the same bridge near to a nature park; after that, if there has been any heavy rain, the road becomes almost impassable in places, so it is advisable to return to the main road at Wilderness and carry on until you pick up the line again, a few miles west of Goukamma at a place called Bleshoender.

There are many outstandingly good locations on this line at which to see and photograph steam. I must make special mention of Kaaimans River bridge, the causeway at Wilderness and at Bleshoender, crossing the lakes near Rondevlie, leaving Goukamma in both directions and the causeway approaching Knysna – to name but a few. There are some good shots to be had of shunting at George station and yards both during the day and at night. It is also well worth a trip on the train; a coach for passengers is attached behind the goods vehicles.

(See photographs Nos. 7, 18, 19, 53, 54, 71, 73, 91.)

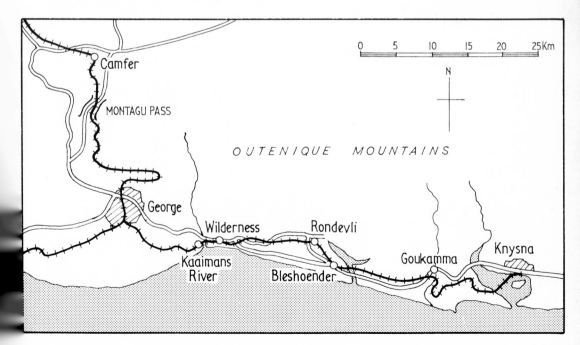

Section 3 – Assegaaibos-Avontuur

This is the steam worked section of the 2ft gauge line from Port Elizabeth and is now entirely worked by Class NG15 2–8–2s of Humewood Road depot, Port Elizabeth, sub-shedded at Assegaaibos and Avontuur. A good road runs near to or by the side of the line for most of the way so that it is quite easy to follow a train by car.

There is usually a departure from Assegaaibos at around 09.00 but it is as well to check on this at the station the previous afternoon as times can vary. By following this departure, which takes around six hours to complete its journey to Avontuur, it is possible to see and photograph eastbound trains which cross the 09.00 train at some of the main stations.

As mentioned in the shed guide, one very interesting feature at Assegaaibos shed is the turntable, a rarity in South Africa as engines usually turn on triangles. It is situated some yards from the shed in the Avontuur direction but is tucked behind some buildings so could easily be missed.

From Assegaaibos the line climbs for most of the way to Joubertina (where trains usually cross), so there are many good shots of westbound trains to be had. However the line drops down just before Joubertina and crosses a river bridge which is an excellent place to photograph eastbound trains. From Joubertina to Avontuur the line runs through the Langkloof valley, passing through many scenic locations.

Between Joubertina and Louterwater the road runs at the side of the valley overlooking the line which now runs through acres of orchards.

The line then comes to Misgund where good photographs are possible in and around the attractive setting of the station. Near to Haarlem the line once again runs through valleys of orchards and from Haarlem the line passes through very pleasant scenery until the terminus is reached at Avontuur.

(See photographs Nos. 10, 12, 35, 36, 52, 80, 82.)

Section 4 – Port Elizabeth Area

A fair number of the Port Elizabeth suburban services are still steam worked by Class 15ARs from Sydenham shed. Most trains run through to Uitenhage but some terminate at New Brighton and Swartkops. Good shots are possible at Port Elizabeth station, from where shunting activities in the docks can also be seen. Between Swartkops and Redhouse the line crosses tidal mud flats making for good photographic possibilities.

There is also scope for good photographs between Redhouse and Perseverance. Particularly recommended are sites in and around Perseverance station. At both ends of the station are fine semaphore signals which add to the atmosphere. Uitenhage is an industrial area but some good station shots are possible here.

On Saturdays only between June and January the Apple Express runs on the 2ft gauge line between Humewood Road station in Port Elizabeth and Loerie and is hauled by a Class 15NG 2–8–2. For good shots on this line one idea would be to travel on the train as there are several photographic stops including one on Van Stadens bridge. However if you do not travel on the train there are some reasonable locations in the suburbs of Port Elizabeth. From Gamtoos near Loerie is the short 2ft gauge line to Patensie.

Some 25 to 30 miles north of Port Elizabeth, on the main line to Alicedale are two steam worked branches to Alexandria and Kirkwood which leave the main line at Barkly Bridge and Addo respectively.

(See photographs Nos. 9, 26, 27, 28, 44, 50, 63, 76, 83, 96, 97.)

Section 5 – Grahamstown Area

Some 80 miles north east of Port Elizabeth is Grahamstown, from which point steam still operates to Alicedale in the west and Port Alfred in the south east. All trains are hauled by Class 19Ds of Grahamstown shed. The Alicedale line has steep gradients in both directions including an eastbound section of 1 in 40 from km post 4 to km post 16. On the Port Alfred section about 13 miles out of Grahamstown, the line crosses the Bloukrans river bridge. This bridge is in a dip so that trains are faced with a climb in each direction.

At Grahamstown station, which is also very photogenic, is a preserved GDA Garratt, No. 2257, these types having been regular performers on this line in the past.

(See photographs Nos. 2, 6, 65, 92.)

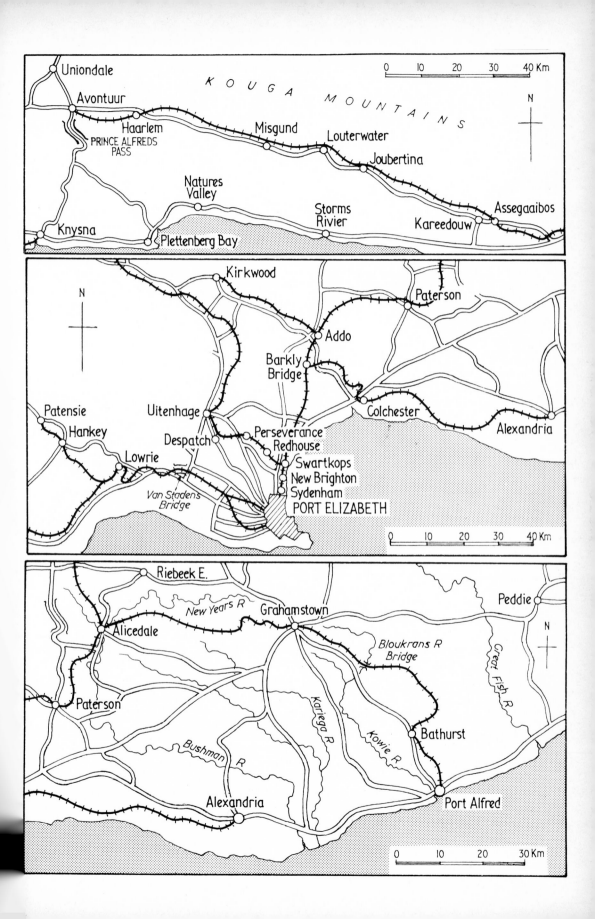

8. Situated at the foot of the Montagu Pass is the town of George, junction for the Knysna branch. Entering the station on the right is a westbound goods hauled by GMA Garratt No 4123, while on the left GMA No 4098, at the head of another goods train, takes water into its supplementary tank wagon before leaving for the long climb over the Montagu pass to Oudtshoorn on 25 July 1979. This line has now gone over to diesel traction.

Section 6 – Sterkstroom-Maclear Branch

This branch, set in the Eastern Cape, runs from the junction of Sterkstroom, on the East London/Queenstown-Burgersdorp/Rosmead lines, and passes through some spectacular scenery before reaching Maclear, a distance of some 174 miles. Motive power for the line is provided by 19Ds. Sterkstroom locomotives work as far as Indwe, from where Indwe based locomotives take over for the journey to Elliot. On the final section trains are worked by locomotives from Maclear. There is a triangle at Elliot where engines are turned.

Gradients are very severe; a few miles out of Sterkstroom, Maclear trains have to negotiate Penhoek pass and this is followed by a steep climb up to Birds River. Later comes another steep climb into Elliot.

Obviously a line like this abounds in good photographic positions and as the trains are fairly slow it is possible to follow by car. When visiting this line I have stayed at Sterkstroom, from where it is possible to photograph the 07.00 goods as far

as Penhoek pass, then return for breakfast, after which the 09.30 passenger can be followed, a train which goes right through to Maclear.

There is also another freight for Indwe leaving Sterkstroom at 13.00, which can be followed to Birds River, where the 08.15 Maclear-Sterkstroom in the opposite direction can then be photographed. A mile or so east of Birds River station is a splendid spot at which to photograph this train, for there is a steep climb into Birds River from the Maclear direction set against a background of distant hills. Also noteworthy is the Tsomo River bridge which the line crosses at Xalanga between Indwe and Elliot.

Other shorter branches in this area still with steam workings are, notably, Molteno-Jamestown, Queenstown-Tarkastad and Queenstown-Qamato.

(See photographs Nos. 21, 22, 46, 49, 67, 81.)

Section 7 – Kimberley-Bloemfontein-Bethlehem

The first section of this single track main line from Kimberley to Bloemfontein is just over 100 miles long and undulates for most of the way,

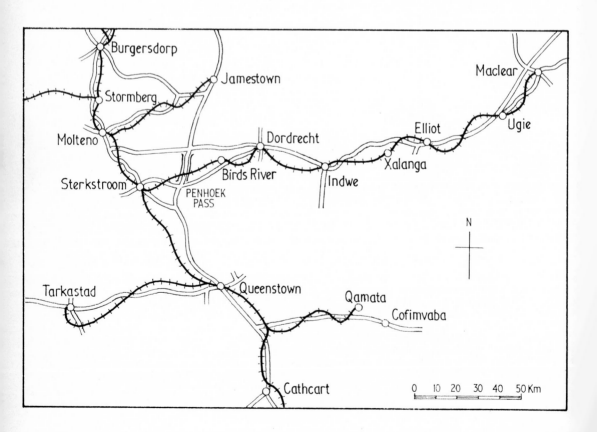

culminating in a five mile climb of 1 in 70 into Kloofeind, a few miles west of Bloemfontein. Motive power for this section and also from Bloemfontein to Bethlehem is provided by Class 25NCs and 15Fs from Kimberley, Bloemfontein and Bethlehem sheds.

Apart from the climbs into Kloofeind from both directions this section of the line is not outstanding for photography, but the second section between Bloemfontein and Bethlehem, 190 miles long, has many good photographic positions and several trains a day.

There are two steam worked branches on this line from Marseilles to Maseru, in Lesotho, and Modderpoort to Ladybrand. The former is usually worked by a 19D stabled at Modderpoort.

From Bloemfontein there are several recommended locations:

Modderrivier bridge just east of Sannaspos;
Thaba-Nchu area;
Between Marseilles and Modderpoort, particularly eastbound trains climbing into Hoogfontein;
Modderpoort station and the branch into Ladybrand;
Modderpoort to Kilmarnock;
The section from Gumtree to Fouriesburg, especially around the Ficksburg area;
Between Fouriesburg and Slabberts;
Slabberts station and surrounding area.

Trains between Bloemfontein and Bethlehem are fairly slow, making it possible to follow by car.

At Harrismith, some 50 miles east of Bethlehem is the short branch to Warden which, on weekdays only, has a return working by a 19D.

(See photographs Nos. 3, 5, 24, 48, 59, 61, 62, 89, 90, 98.)

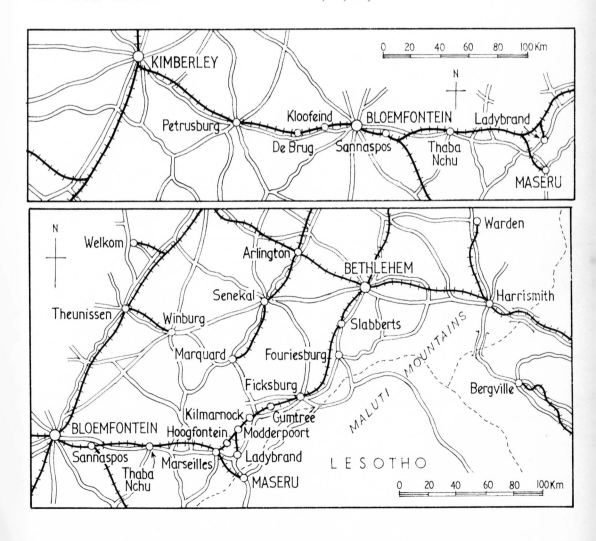

Section 8 – Natal (2ft gauge and industrial)

There are five 2ft gauge lines in Natal:

    Port Shepstone-Harding
    Umzinto-Ixopo-Donnybrook
    Estcourt-Weenan
    Ixopo-Madonela
    Umlaas Road-Mid Illovo

All are worked by Garratts of Class NGG16 and a few of the earlier and similar Class NGG13.

Of the five lines the first three are the most interesting, Ixopa-Madonela being a short branch off the Donnybrook line and Umlaas Road-Mid Illovo now having very little traffic.

The scenery on the Port Shepstone line is good but road access, particularly the Harding end of the line, can be difficult. The best section from the photographic point of view is just out of Port Shepstone, where the line runs against the background of the Indian Ocean.

Umzinto-Donnybrook is possibly the most scenic line of all as well as being the busiest. A good road follows the line for most of the way thus giving easy access to the many fine photographic locations. Horseshoe curves abound on this line, especially the area around Highflats (where trains are booked to meet either to exchange locomotives or crews).

The Estcourt-Weenan line is fairly short but good shots are possible of trains leaving Weenan station and near to Weenan where the road runs by the trackside. A further attraction is the blue liveried NGG13 2–6–2+2–6–2 No. 59 which works on this line.

The northern part of the province is still rich in coal reserves and quite a few of the collieries, especially in the Vryheid and Newcastle areas, are steam worked. Of particular note are the Enyati Colliery and Vryheid Coronation Colliery at Vryheid, Hlobane Colliery at Hlobane and Umgala Colliery at Utrecht. Motive power is very varied and includes many ex SAR and former Rhodesian Railways locomotives.

(See photographs Nos. 13, 29, 30, 31, 32, 69, 70, 86, 87.)

Section 9 – Transvaal Area

Although there is still a fair amount of steam working in the Transvaal it is spread over a large area. With this in mind it is probably better to concentrate on lines that are reasonably near to each other and have fairly interesting workings.

The Springs-Breyten line is now fairly well dieselised but there is still a certain amount of trip working around Springs, Bethel and Breyten by 15Fs and a few 12ARs. There are also steam worked branches in this area from Bethel to Volkrust, Standerton to Vrede and Breyten to Lothair, the first two being worked by 19Ds and the last by Class 24s. Also worth a visit is Waterval Boven where quite a number of GMA Garratts are to be seen, most of them stored, but a few still shunt in the yard and do trip workings in the area.

Although the Rayton-Cullinan branch is quite short, it is worth a visit to see the Class 15CAs at work on passenger trains. These engines are reputed to be the noisiest in South Africa. Several good locations are to be found on this line. One spot is about two miles out of Rayton, going towards Cullinan, where the line crosses the road. Around here by varying position it is possible to photograph trains in both directions in reasonably attractive settings. Other locations are in and around Cullinan station, the line here climbing towards Rayton. These trains actually run from Eerste Fabrieke on weekdays and from Pretoria on Saturdays only. However as the Pretoria to Witbank line is now under the wires I have concentrated on the Rayton to Cullinan section which is not electrified.

Industrial steam is still in abundance in the Witbank coalfield area where a variety of ex SAR as well as industrial locomotives can be seen working at many collieries and exchange sidings.

(See photographs Nos. 14, 15, 16, 17, 33, 37, 45, 51, 72, 79, 84, 85.)

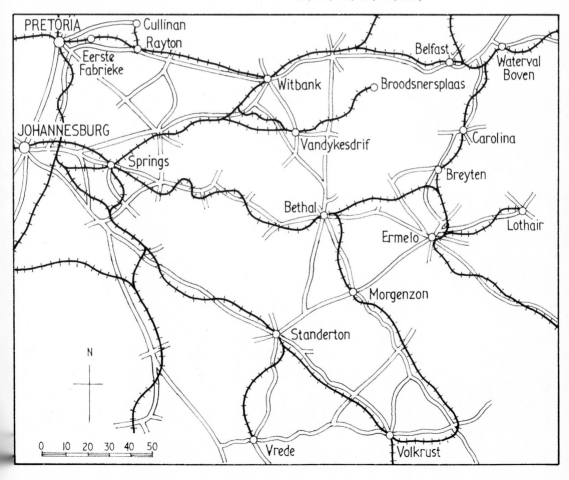

9. *Top left:* The early evening of 27 July 1979 sees a busy scene at Port Elizabeth docks with 15ARs engaged in shunting duties.

10. *Left:* A pair of Class NG15 2ft gauge 2–8–2s Nos 118 and 124 at Assegaaibos shed on the evening of 27 July 1976.

11. *Above:* Northbound freights headed by Class 25NC 4–8–4s Nos 3531 *Tania* and 3517 *Janice* receive attention at Orange River before leaving for Kimberley in August 1979.

12. Class NG15 2–8–2s Nos 146 and 120 make a splendid sight as they round a curve west of Joubertina with a ballast train bound for Assegaaibos on 23 July 1980.

13. With driver Bill Bester in charge, seated outside the cab, Class NGG13 2–6–2 + 2–6–2 No 78 makes a spirited start out of Weenan with the 08.15 to Estcourt on 1 August 1980. This 2ft gauge Garratt was built by Hanomag in 1928. The outside cab seats with a flap extension to the roof on these 2ft gauge engines give the crew more air than they would get inside on a hot day.

14. Three 15CA 4–8–2s and a 15F 4–8–2 make a splendid quartet at Capitol Park shed Pretoria on 8 August 1980.

15. Also at Capitol Park shed on the same day was 15F No 3035, built by North British, and 19D No 2650 built by Krupp.

16. Pausing between shunting duties at Landau Colliery
near Witbank is 4–8–2 No 2 built by North British.
Tender numbering often causes confusion; Landau
No 3 was a former SAR Class 3BR. Photographed on
5 August 1980.

17. Still earning its keep at Apex Mines Ltd (Greenside
Colliery) near Witbank is a former SAR Class 1A
4–8–0 built by North British in 1909.

18. Class 24 No 3624 throws out a fine exhaust as it climbs out of Goukamma with a Knysna–George train on 24 July 1979. Note the smokebox ornamentation.

19. Another scene near Goukamma, this time with sister engine No 3622 *Rosie*, approaching the rock cutting before entering the station with a Knysna train.

20. *Top left:* A pair of 15ARs climb out of Aliwal North with a freight for Burgersdorp on 5 August 1976.

21. *Left:* Class 19D No 2712 threads the bleak open country at Penhoek Pass with the midday Sterkstroom to Indwe goods train on 30 July 1979.

22. *Above:* Also climbing through Penhoek Pass on 30 July is the morning Sterkstroom–Maclear passenger train hauled by a 19D 4–8–2.

23. *Top left:* Class 25NCs Nos 3436 *Anne* and 3521 storm out of Orange River with a northbound goods on 28 July 1980.

24. *Bottom left:* An evening passenger train bound for Bloemfontein leaves Marseilles with Class 25NC No 3403 in charge in July 1980.

25. *Above:* The shadows lengthen as Class 25NC No 3436 *Anne* races through Kraankuil with a Kimberley–De Aar goods on 28 July 1980.

26. *Below:* Class 15AR No 2096 built by Maffei, darkens the sky as it pulls out of Perseverance with a Port Elizabeth to Uitenhage train on 25 July 1980.

Night time at Port Elizabeth station, 27 July 1979.

27. Close look at the cab of Class 24 No 3628, after
bringing in a suburban train.

28. Waiting to leave with the 20.38 to Uitenhage is a
    15AR 4–8–2.

Four scenes on the Umzinto–Donnybrook line in Natal on 8/9 August 1976.

29. Class NGG16 2ft gauge Garratts slumber at Umzinto shed.

30. NGG16 No 129, built by Beyer Peacock, is seen at work rounding a horseshoe curve near Highflats with an Ixopo bound goods.

31. Another shot of the previous train, this time between Braemar and Highflats.

32. With a load of wood bound for Umzinto, a Class NGG16 Garratt descends cautiously round reverse curves near Highflats.

33. Class 15CA No 2857 takes water at Cullinan station before leaving with the afternoon train to Rayton and Eerste Fabrieke on the eastern approach to Pretoria on 6 August 1980.

34. A pair of class 25NCs, led by No 3424 *Marjorie* make a fine sight as they storm out of Modder River with a morning Kimberley–De Aar goods on 3 August 1979. New points and crossings lie alongside ready for relaying.

35. and 36. Two views of Class NG15 2–8–2 No 121,
    built by Franco–Belge in 1949, shunting in
    Assegaaibos yard on the Port Elizabeth–Avontuur
    line on the morning of 23 July 1980.

37. Springbok Colliery near Witbank is the setting as No 1, a 4–8–2 tender tank engine, originally a conventional tank engine, but now with side tanks removed, hauls a load of empties back to the colliery yard from the exchange sidings on 6 August 1980. This engine was built by North British in 1948.

38. Class 14CR 4–8–2 No 1897, built by Montreal in 1919, does some late evening shunting at Riversdale on the Worcester–Mossel Bay line on 25 July 1976.

39. *Above:* Reflections at Vorbaii shed, Mossel Bay. Class GMA Garratt No 4113 *Heidi*, built by North British, receives attention before leaving shed to take out a goods to Oudtshoorn, a trip which involves the long climb over the famous Montagu pass. 25 July 1979.

40. *Top right:* GMA Garratt No 4125, built by Beyer Peacock in 1958, is pictured here at Riversdale in the Western Cape on 26 July 1976.

41. *Right:* Class 25 4–8–4 condensing locomotive No 3508 at Beaconsfield shed, Kimberley on 4 August 1976. In recent years as these locomotives have been displaced from areas with poor water supplies the need for condensers has diminished; the class has been rebuilt without the equipment and is similar to the 25NC locomotives but with round tops to the tender tanks.

42. *Top left:* Preserved Class 5R Pacific No 781 at De Aar shed on 1 August 1979. This engine was the only one of its class and is fitted with Stephenson link motion and long travel valves.

43. *Left:* Also to be seen at De Aar shed is this veteran Class 6A 4–6–0, No 462, built around the end of the last century, plus vintage coach. 27 July 1980.

44. *Above:* About to depart from Port Elizabeth's Humewood Road station is the Apple Express headed by 2ft gauge 2–8–2 No 124. This train runs on Saturdays only between June and January.

45. Class 15CA No 2836, built by North British, climbs a
grade near Cullinan with an afternoon train from
Eerste Fabrieke on 12 August 1976.

46. The early morning sun glints on Class 19D No 2768
as it climbs through Penhoek Pass with the 07.00
Sterkstroom to Indwe freight on 30 July 1979.

47. A pair of Class 15Fs Nos 2974 and 3010 pull out of Newcastle with coal empties for Utrecht on 11 August 1976. Before dieselisation in 1978, this line was noted for the standard of its 15F locomotives.

48. This scene, reminiscent of the American West, shows an immaculate class 25NC, No 3403, of Bethlehem shed with a Bloemfontein–Bethlehem train. The location is Sekonyela near Ficksburg and the date is 30 July 1980.

49. *Right:* Class 19D No 2511 waits in Sterkstroom station while the coaches are washed down before leaving with the morning passenger train to Maclear on 31 July 1979.

50. *Below:* An immaculate 15AR No 2011 hurries along near North End in the suburbs of Port Elizabeth with a local train to Uitenhage on 30 July 1976.

51. *Bottom right:* Class 15CA No 2836 receives attention at Cullinan station before leaving with an afternoon train to Eerste Fabrieke on 12 August 1976.

52. *Top left:* NG15 No 148, a 2ft gauge 2–8–2 built by Henschel, pulls out of Kompan-Jiesdrif, situated between Joubertina and Assegaaibos, with an Assegaaibos train on 28 July 1976.

53. *Left:* Class 24 2–8–4 No 3622 is caught by a long lens as it crosses the lakes near Rondevlei with a George–Knysna train. The prominent shape of the Vanderbuilt tender stands out. 26 July 1979.

54. *Above:* The midday train to George, headed by Class 24 No 3624, leaves Knysna on 24 July 1979.

55. Rebuilt Class 25NC No 3503 *Tania* hurries through the scrubland near Kraankuil, on the Kimberley–De Aar main line with a southbound goods on 29 July 1980. This is a former condensing locomotive and the round top rebuilt tender will be noted.

56. Another Kraankuil scene, this time very near to the station. A pair of former condensing Class 25NCs led by 3465 *Carol*, thunder through with a southbound freight on 2 August 1979.

57. *Top left:* A 19D and a pair of 15ARs make a fine sight as they simmer at Rosmead shed on 1 August 1976.

58. *Left:* A GMA Garratt contrasts with Class 12A No 1547 at De Aar shed on 1 August 1979. The Garratt was en route from the Cape Western area (having been replaced there by diesel traction) to Zimbabwe, where several of these engines are now working.

59. *Above:* 15F No 2963, built by North British, comes face to face with Borsig-built 19D No 2703. The location is Modderpoort and the date 4 August 1979.

60. Class 19D No 2769 darkens the sky as it climbs through the main street of Fauresmith with a Koffiefontein to Springfontein train on 3 August 1979.

61. Conversation piece at Modderpoort. Class 15F No 2963 prepares to leave with a freight for Bloemfontein on 4 August 1979.

62. *Top left:* The evening sun glints on 19D No 2769 as it pulls out of Marseilles at the head of a train bound for Maseru in Lesotho on 29 July 1980.

63. *Left:* A local train from Uitenhage to Port Elizabeth leaves Perseverance hauled by 15AR No 2017 on 30 July 1976.

64. *Above:* A westbound passenger train, hauled by a GMA Garratt, climbs into Skimmelkrans, situated between George and Mossel Bay on the Port Elizabeth to Cape Town line on 26 July 1979.

65. *Above:* Waiting to leave Grahamstown on a Port Alfred train is Class 19D No 2750. 28 July 1979.

66. *Top right:* 25NC No 3423 *Victoria* makes a fine display of smoke as it pulls out of Belmont, junction for the branch to Douglas, with a De Aar to Kimberley passenger train on 27 July 1979.

67. *Right:* A Queenstown to Burgersdorp goods headed by 19D No 2100 enters Sterkstroom station on the afternoon of 29 July 1979.

68. *Above:* Beaconsfield shed, Kimberley, 4 August 1976. Class 24 No 3602 is seen shunting the coaling stage.

69. *Below:* NGG16 No 129, one of a batch built by Beyer Peacock in 1951, receives attention at Highflats station on the Umzinto–Donnybrook line on 9 August 1976.

70. *Right:* After working in from Weenan, Class NGG13 Garratt No 78 is pictured here at Estcourt shed where it will be serviced before leaving with the afternoon return working. 1 August 1980.

71. The Indian Ocean forms the background to a Knysna–George train as it crosses the Kaaimans River bridge hauled by a Class 24 2–8–4 on 25 July 1979.

72. Witbank Colliery's No 2, a 4–8–2 built by North British, storms along near the engine shed with a load of coal for the exchange sidings on 5 August 1980.

73. Class 24 No 3622 *Rosie* is pictured here rounding a tight curve between Wilderness and Rondevlei with a George–Knysna train on 25 July 1979.

74. *Top left:* Approaching Burgersdorp in the Eastern Cape is the afternoon goods from Aliwal North hauled by Class 15ARs Nos 1810 and 2013 on 5 August 1976.

75. *Left:* Topping the climb over the Lootsberg Pass with a Rosmead to Graaff Reinet goods on 2 August 1976 is 19D No 2643, built by Krupp in 1938. The lines in the foreground are part of the triangle which enabled banking engines to turn before returning to Rosmead.

76. *Above:* Class 24 No 3604 pulls out of Kinkelbos station, near Colchester, with an Alexandria to Port Elizabeth train on 26 July 1980.

77. *Top left:* GMA No 4082 waits to leave Skimmelkrans with a Mossel Bay to George train on 26 July 1976.

78. *Left:* Starting out of Rosmead, on the long climb over the Lootsberg Pass, with a De Aar to Graaff Reinet train is GMA No 4080. 1 August 1976.

79. *Above:* S2 0–8–0 No 3769, built by Krupp in 1952, is seen shunting at Waterval Boven shed on 4 August 1980. This class of 100 locomotives was subject to severe weight restrictions on light rail in harbours, hence the small boiler. A number of GMA Garratts are stored at this shed.

85. *Top left:* 15CA No 2857 pulls out of Rayton with an afternoon train to Cullinan on 6 August 1980.

86. *Left:* Near Highflats with an Umzinto to Ixopo goods is a class NGG16 2–6–2 + 2–6–2 2ft gauge Garratt. 9 August 1976.

87. *Above:* The 08.15 to Estcourt climbs out of Weenan hauled by class NGG13 No 78 on 1 August 1980.

90. *Left:* The rugged mountainous country around Fouriesburg provides an attractive backcloth for 15F No 3124 on a Bloemfontein to Bethlehem passenger train. The location is midway between Fouriesburg and Sheridan. 4 August 1979.

Previous Page

88. *Left:* Originally built as a condensing locomotive but now rebuilt, 25NC No 3517 *Janice*, blasts out of Orange River with a De Aar to Kimberley goods on 2 August 1979.

89. *Right:* 15F No 2948, built by North British in 1939, shunts at Marseilles before leaving with an evening goods to Bloemfontein on 29 July 1980.

91. Class 24 No 3624 hurries through an attractive woodland setting just west of Goukamma with the midday Knysna–George train on 24 July 1979.

92. On the afternoon of 28 July 1979 a class 19D is bus shunting at Grahamstown station.

93. *Top left:* On 1 August 1979 class 25NC 3434 *Corry* storms along the De Aar–Kimberley line with a southbound goods. The location is the rock cutting just north of Potfontein station.

94. *Left:* 25NC 4–8–4 No 3431 *Lindy Lou* climbs out of Poupan with a De Aar–Kimberley passenger train on 28 July 1980.

95. *Above:* A pair of former condensing 25NCs, led by No 3491 *Sandie*, climb the steep grade through Belmont with a De Aar to Kimberley goods on 2 August 1979.

Morning and Evening at Port Elizabeth.

96. A Class 15AR 4–8–2 pauses between shunting duties on the evening of 27 July 1979.

97. 15AR No 2082 makes a spirited departure with mid-morning train to Uitenhage.

98. The late evening sun highlights 15F No 3124 as it
pulls out of Slabberts with a Bloemfontein to
Bethlehem train on 4 August 1979.